CHILDREN'S AND PARENTS' SERVICES
PATCHOGUE-MEDFORD LIBRARY

If you have a home computer with Internet access you may:

- request an item to be placed on hold.
- renew an item that is not overdue or on hold.
- view titles and due dates checked out on your card.
- view and/or pay your outstanding fines online (over $5).

To view your patron record from your home computer click on
Patchogue-Medford Library's homepage: www.pmlib.org

MAKING ART WITH FABRIC

Gillian Chapman & Pam Robson

PowerKiDS press.

New York

All projects should be done carefully, with an adult's help and supervision v

appropriate (especially for activities involving any cutting, carving, or sewing

adult should execute or supervise any work with a craft knife, and safety scis

should be used for all cutting.

Published in 2008 by The Rosen Publishing Group, Inc.
29 East 21st Street, New York, NY 10010

Copyright© 2008 Wayland/The Rosen Publishing Group, Inc.

First Edition

Picture Acknowledgments
Ecoscene 4t (Ian Beames);
Eye Ubiquitous 4b (John Hulme); Link 5b (Orde Eliason)
Zefa 5t

Library of Congress Cataloging-in-Publication Data

Chapman, Gillian.
  Making art with fabric / Gillian Chapman & Pam Robson. -- 1st ed.
     p. cm. -- (Everyday art)
  Includes index.
  ISBN-13: 978-1-4042-3722-3 (library binding)
  ISBN-10: 1-4042-3722-4 (library binding)
  1. Textile crafts--Juvenile literature. 2. Recycling (Waste, etc.)--Juvenil‹
literature. I. Title.
  TT699.C478 2007
  746--dc22

                                        2006028303

*Ninety-five per cent of the materials used for the projects
in this book were salvaged scraps and remnants*

Manufactured in China

Contents

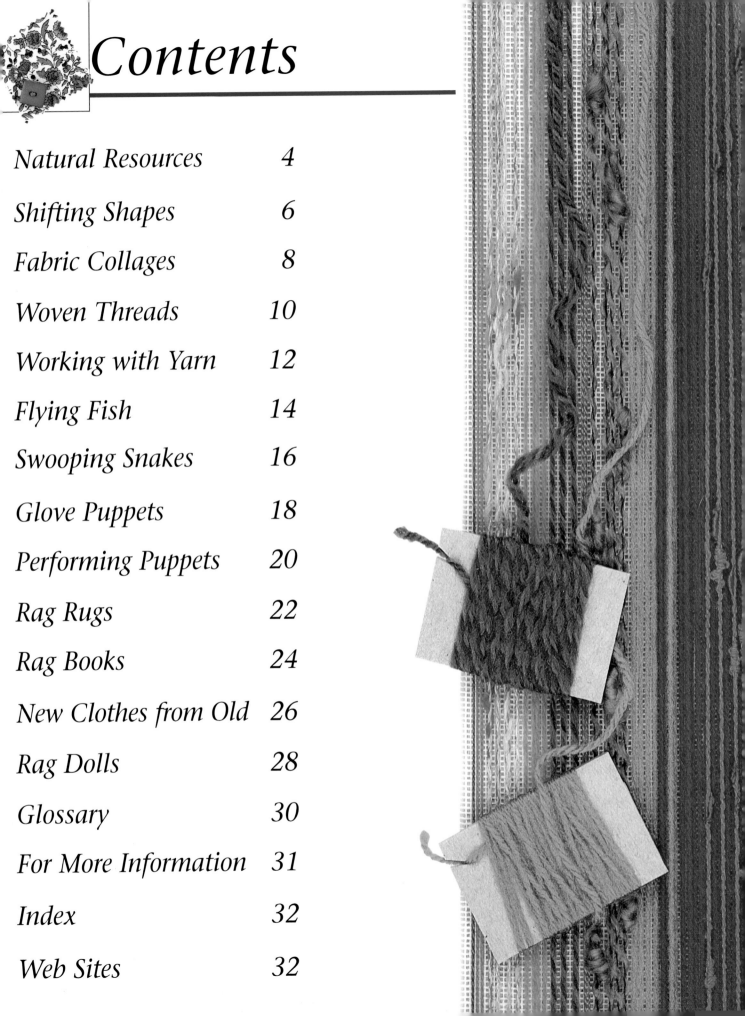

Natural Resources 4

Shifting Shapes 6

Fabric Collages 8

Woven Threads 10

Working with Yarn 12

Flying Fish 14

Swooping Snakes 16

Glove Puppets 18

Performing Puppets 20

Rag Rugs 22

Rag Books 24

New Clothes from Old 26

Rag Dolls 28

Glossary 30

For More Information 31

Index 32

Web Sites 32

Natural Resources

Fibers and Threads

Human beings have always made use of common natural resources for making materials. Animals like sheep and goats provide fleece and hair for wool. Skins for leather also come from animals. Silk comes from the silkworm. Plants give us fibers, like cotton and linen, which can be spun and woven into cloth.

To produce a new fabric usually means using natural resources to supply and make the yarn. These natural resources can never be replaced. By reusing rags and remnants, you can help conserve the Earth's energy resources. You can also reduce the size of local landfill sites by recycling old garments.

Recycling Fabrics

Poverty has always forced people to reuse or recycle clothing and cloth remnants. In some developing countries, often the only available materials are discarded items. Today, it is essential that every one of us should make the best use of all such materials, because the Earth's natural resources are quickly disappearing.

Litter collects in places the world over. Four percent of this is old clothing. By sorting this waste into recyclable and nonrecyclable groups of materials, we can use many of our throwaway items again. Recycled nylon waste, for example, can be made into tennis balls, and old garments into carpet underlay.

Local people sort garbage at a dump in Bangkok, Thailand, to collect items that can be re-used or recycled.

Collecting

For the projects in this book, you can look for remnants of fabric at yard sales and charity shops. Look around at home and select any old clothing or household fabrics. Make sure you use only clean materials. Remove any buttons or zippers, since these can be reused. Woolen items can be unraveled. Small scraps of cloth are useful for collage, appliqué, and patchwork.

Small remnants of fabric are sewn together to make patchwork quilts. Designs are often traditional.

A scarecrow made from cast-off clothing and fabric remnants. This scarecrow was used to protect crops in a field in Southern Africa.

New from Old

Today, there is a great demand for the work of craftspeople who rely upon recycled objects and materials for inspiration. Creativity depends upon the resources available. It is possible to create beauty out of waste.

Quilts known as *khols* are made from *chindi* — rags collected and sorted by the poor in India. In Bangladesh, quilts known as *kanthas* were traditionally made from scraps and unpicked threads of worn-out saris and dhotis. A kantha is often given as a wedding gift.

In Thailand, scraps of cloth are used to make oven gloves and toys. Silk cocoons are dyed and shaped into flowers. A slipper-sock knitting project employs hundreds of refugees in Pakistan, using unraveled wool from secondhand knitted garments. Cotton scraps are used to make Indian festival decorations. Cotton rags can be used to make paper.

Shifting Shapes

Shape and Size

When you gather together discarded fabrics and clothing, you will find a variety of small decorative items and fasteners, like buttons, beads, and buckles, that can be removed. Look at their different shapes. Some will be curved, others will be angular. They will be made from a range of materials — colored plastic buttons, metal zippers, and fasteners, wooden and glass beads. Sizes will vary from enormous to tiny, depending on the garments that they have been taken from.

Color Wheel

A Typical Collection of Discarded Fabrics and Trimmings

Fabric Color Wheel

Look carefully at all the items in your collection. You have probably found lots of different fabric remnants — scraps of yarn, patches of denim, and pieces of felt. Trimmings may include lace, cords, ribbons, tapes, and old shoelaces. Perhaps you have found an odd sock or glove, or an old belt buckle. You can begin by organizing your collection into a color wheel.

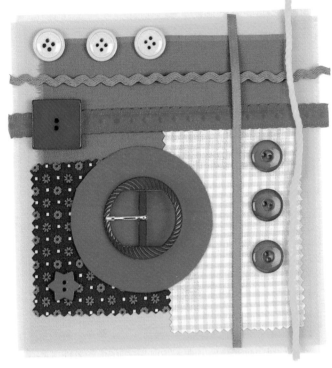

Moving Patterns

Now arrange some of the items to create a temporary collage. Move the objects around until you find the pattern that you like best. You will discover many interesting ways to position the same articles.

Shifting Shapes

Make a series of patterns, using background materials of different colors and textures. Take a photograph, or sketch each one before rearranging.

Collage Arrangements (above and left)

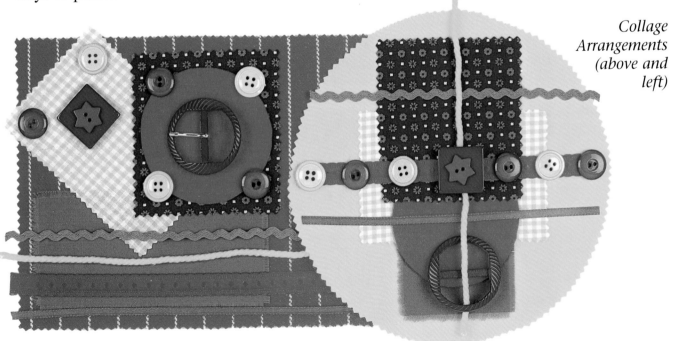

7

Fabric Collages

Color and Texture

All fabrics, whether they are natural or manufactured, have their own special properties. Silk is lightweight and smooth to the touch, but wool feels rough. Woven silk fabric is shiny. Woolen cloth has a matt finish and is used to make garments to keep us warm. Feel the fabrics in your collection — which are rough and which are smooth? Look at them — which are shiny and which are matt?

Woven or Nonwoven

Most fabrics are woven on a loom, but there are some that are nonwoven. Felt is made by compression using heat and moisture. A nonwoven fabric will not fray. Fabrics that fray easily can be difficult to use. For a fabric collage, try to choose materials like felt. Some fabrics, like burlap, are loosely woven, and are hard and stiff. Other woven fabrics, like polyester, a manufactured fabric, are soft and delicate.

Underwater Collage

Fabric Collage

Make a fabric collage using as many colored, textured materials as you can. Plan the design first by sketching a picture the same size as your finished collage. Cut your sketch into separate parts to use as patterns. Find a large piece of strong fabric or cardboard backing. You may decide to glue your collage to the backing cloth, or sew the pieces into place.

Arrange the collage pieces following your sketch. If your picture is a landscape or an underwater scene, choose fabrics suited to the subject. Overlap silky materials and netting. Fray and ripple the fabric to create a wavy effect. If you have yarns, trimmings, and buttons that match your color scheme, use them for details.

You can create an abstract collage by arranging the fabrics according to color or texture. Place warm or cool colors together, or grade them from light to dark.

*Color Collage
(right)*

*Extra Collage
Materials*

Woven Threads

Spiders' Webs

Spiders are skilled at weaving. The ancient Greek story of Arachne tells how she and the goddess Athena took part in a weaving competition. Arachne was turned into a spider by the jealous Athena because her weaving was the best. Scientists who wish to make lightweight fabric strong enough to protect against bullets are experimenting with genetic engineering using spiders' silk genes.

Warp and Weft

Warp threads lie lengthwise along a roll of cloth. They are the downward threads on a loom. Weft threads are woven in and out across the downward warp threads. Stretchy warp threads are best, because they must be pulled taut. Threads that do not stretch will snap under tension.

Looms

Weavers work on a frame called a *loom*. Materials woven on a loom are many and varied, particularly woolen cloth. Many woolen goods have a fluffy surface, because the fibers lie in all directions. Worsted cloth is smooth because the woolen fibers are combed in the same direction.

Collecting Threads

Make a collection of different threads pulled from a variety of fabrics and materials. See if you can identify them. Are they wool, cotton, linen, or polyester? Are they synthetic or natural? Find a piece of loosely woven fabric, such as burlap. Carefully pull out a number of the weft threads. Weave threads from your collection into the burlap to make a colorful new fabric.

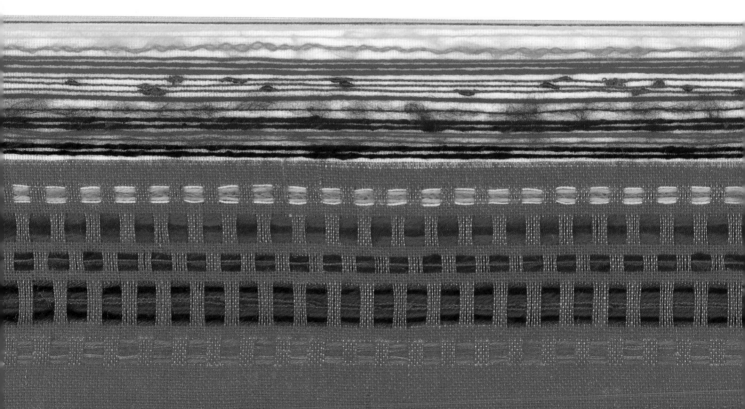

Making a Sunburst

You can make a simple loom. Ask an adult to bend a wire coat hanger into a circle. Overlap the ends and tie the joint with thread. Cover the wire loop with long threads or narrow strips of fabric. Tie threads across the circle and weave other threads in and out, as shown here. Use different textures and thicknesses to create a colorful effect. Finally, decorate the Sunburst with trimmings, such as buttons, beads, and feathers, and hang it up.

use blanket stitch to cover the wire

tie joint with thread

Finished Sunbursts

Weaving Threads (left)

11

Working with Yarn

Weaving Traditions

In Africa, weaving traditions vary a great deal. In North Africa, it is the women who do the weaving. In West Africa and East Africa, it is more likely to be the men. Many different types of looms are used. Today, traditional cloths are being replaced by factory-produced fabrics.

Kente cloth, woven from strips of rayon or silk, made by the Asante peoples of Ghana, was once made only for kings. In Malaysia, Songket cloth weaving is an ancient craft. Traditional patterns are woven in gold and silver threads. The finished cloth is worn by Malaysians on ceremonial occasions.

Unraveling Hand Knits

Unraveling Yarn

Unwanted knitted garments can easily be taken apart. The unraveled yarn is crinkly, and this can give an interesting texture to your projects. Choose only clean hand knits, in good condition. Wind the different yarns on cardboard bobbins, separating the colors. You can use this yarn for a weaving project.

Making Pom-Poms

These yarns can also be used to make colorful pom-poms. To make a pom-pom, cut two cardboard circles the same size. Cut a hole in the middle of both circles. Wind the yarn through the two rings until the central hole is full. Carefully cut the wound yarn at the edge of the cardboard. Tie strong thread between the rings, and knot it tightly before cutting the cardboard pieces to remove them.

cutting

card shape

winding

Making Pom-Poms

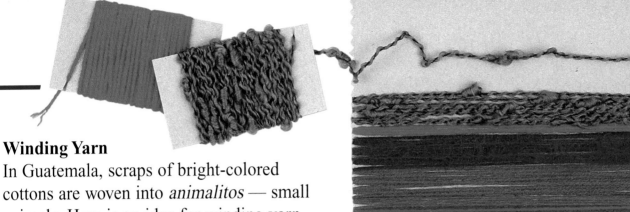

Winding Yarn

In Guatemala, scraps of bright-colored cottons are woven into *animalitos* — small animals. Here is an idea for winding yarn scraps around pieces of cardboard to make these animal pictures.

Winding Wool on Cardboard

You will need a piece of thick cardboard and a selection of yarns. Make small notches in the sides of the cardboard to fasten the ends of each piece of wool. Wind the yarn around the cardboard, choosing different colors and textures to create a striped effect.

Find a piece of fabric the same size as the cardboard, and cut an animal shape in the middle. Place the fabric over the top of the weaving, so that the colored stripes are visible through the animal-shaped hole. Sew or glue the fabric frame to the cardboard.

Elephant Stencil Made from Fabric

Finished Elephant Picture

Add fabric features such as ears.

Decorate the fabric with colored stitching.

13

Flying Fish

Fish and Dragons

Wind socks were used by soldiers to find out wind strength and direction for their archers and also to frighten the enemy. In 1066, when the Normans invaded Britain, the Anglo-Saxon banner was a dragon-shaped wind sock. Historians think it is so because it can be seen on the Bayeux Tapestry (a piece of cloth decorated with scenes from the Battle of Hastings, 1066).

In Japan, the Boys' Festival is celebrated on the fifth day of the fifth month. Families with male children fly a bright-colored wind sock from the roof. The most popular shape is the carp. This fish struggles to swim upstream each year, and it symbolizes the boy's journey through life.

Making a Carp Wind sock

Lightweight Materials

A wind sock must blow easily in the wind and should be made from durable, lightweight materials. Synthetic fabrics like nylon and polyester have these properties. Old sheets and shirts are most suitable for the purpose.

To make a wind sock, you will need a large piece of fabric, such as a nylon sheet, and smaller scraps of colored material for decoration. The wind sock acts as a wind tunnel, open at both ends. Look at pictures of traditional Japanese wind socks. Use these to sketch your design.

Cutting out the Shape

Follow your design and cut out two body shapes from the sheet. Pin and sew them together. You should always be careful when using and storing needles.

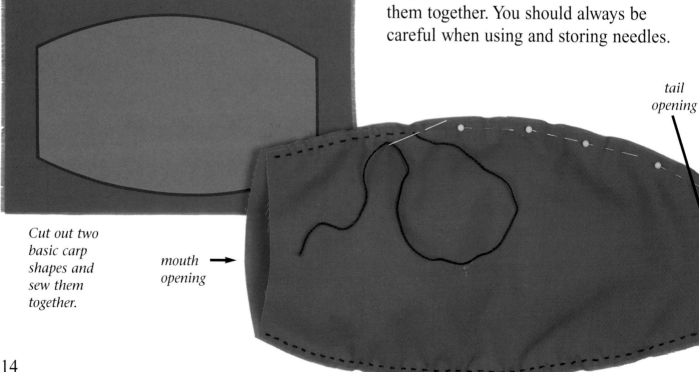

Cut out two basic carp shapes and sew them together.

mouth → opening

tail opening

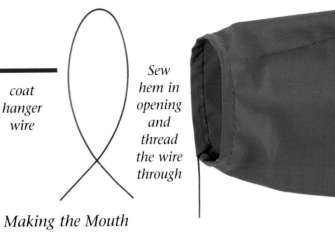

coat
hanger
wire

Sew
hem in
opening
and
thread
the wire
through

Making the Mouth

Making a Wind Sock

Make a hem in the mouth opening through which to thread a piece of coat hanger wire. Ask and adult to help you twist the two ends of the wire together to make a loop. This will keep the mouth open.

Decorate the wind sock by glueing or sewing pieces of material to the body. Overlap circle shapes for scales, and make pleated fins and a tail.

Tie three pieces of cord to the wire loop and attach these securely to a strong stick. Now find a high and exposed place to fix your wind sock.

*Fabric Circles
and Pleats for
Decoration*

Finished Carp Wind Sock

15

Swooping Snakes

Chinese Kites

Kites existed in China as early as the fifth century B.C. They were flown for both pleasure and for military purposes. Kites shaped like mythical birds and dragons were common. Many had rolling eyes and moving tails. Some whistled as they flew and were used to frighten enemies. Kite flying did not reach Europe until the sixteenth century.

Materials for Kites

A kite must be light and easy to manage. It must also be strong. The materials to make a kite need to be lightweight and durable. In ancient times, the Chinese used silk or paper for their kites, but paper is not durable. Today, synthetic fabrics like nylon and polyester can be used.

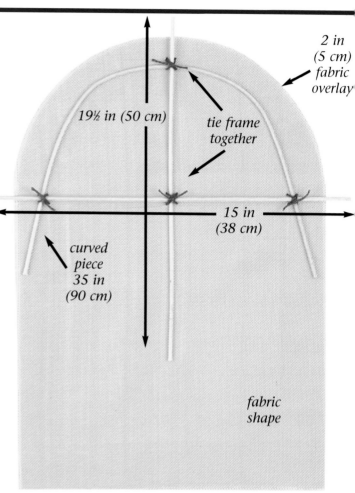

Making the Bamboo Frame

Attaching Fabric to the Frame

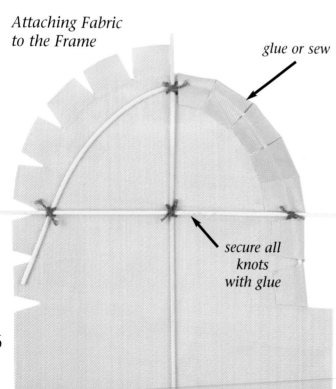

A Snake Kite

This snake kite is simple to make. Because of its flat head and long tail, it can fly in the lightest breeze. Choose lightweight materials to make the kite, and decorate it with scraps of colored fabric or paper.

Making the Frame

The frame is made from three pieces of flexible bamboo. Ask an adult to cut to the following sizes: 1 x 19½ in (50 cm), 1 x 15 in (38 cm) and 1 x 35 in (90 cm). Have an adult help you assemble the frame by tying the pieces together as shown in the diagram above.

Attaching the Body

Choose a large piece of strong, lightweight fabric for the head. It will need to be larger than the bamboo frame. Place the frame on top of the fabric, as shown opposite. Cut the fabric to the shape of the frame leaving a 2 in (5 cm) overlap all around. Glue or sew the fabric to the frame. Secure all knots and bindings with blobs of glue to make them extra strong.

Overlap fabric circles for the tail.

Finished Snake Kite

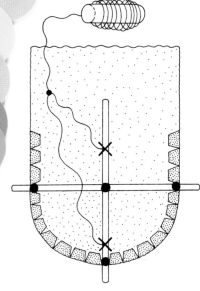

Attaching the Strings

Making the Tail

The tail is made from overlapping circles of fabric or paper. Begin by glueing them to the head, and extend the kite by making the tail as long as you like.

Attaching the Strings

It is important to make sure the strings are balanced and attached firmly to the kite. Use a strong nylon thread and follow the stringing diagram above.

Be careful when you fly your snake kite. Make sure an adult is nearby and that you do not stand close to overhead power lines or trees.

17

Glove Puppets

Traditional Puppets

Puppeteering is an ancient skill common to many cultures. The oldest type of puppeteering began in India, where rod and hand puppet performances were popular forms of entertainment. Hand puppets are perhaps the simplest to make and the easiest to operate. They are often found in countries that have strong traditions of storytelling, where they are used to bring a story to life.

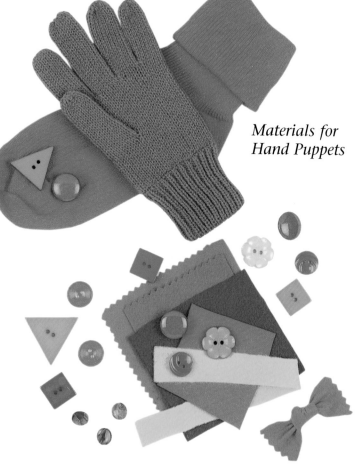

Materials for Hand Puppets

Marking the Position of Features

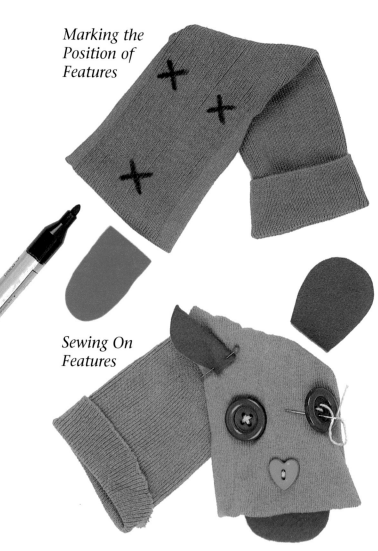

Sewing On Features

Making Hand Puppets

If you have odd socks, mittens, and gloves in your collection of scrap, they can be turned into puppet characters.

Place your hand inside a sock, with your fingers in the toe and thumb in the heel. Push in the sole of the sock to form the puppet's mouth. Using a black felt-tip pen, mark where the eyes, nose, and ears should be positioned.

Cut out ears and a tongue from scraps of fabric and sew them into place. Use buttons and beads for the nose and eyes.

Other Ideas

Odd gloves and mittens can also be made into puppets. Push in the middle fingers and thumb of an old glove. Stuff the first and little finger with small fabric scraps to make ears for your puppet, then add the other features.

Use Old Gloves and Mittens

Making a Puppet Theater

To make a puppet theater, find a strong cardboard box, large enough for the puppets to move inside. Cut a hole in the front of the box for the stage. Operate the puppets through a smaller hole cut in the back.

Decorating the Theater

Cover the box with material and decorate it with fabric scraps and trimmings. Make some curtains and scenery, attaching them to the inside of the theater. Write a short play for all your hand puppet characters.

Puppet Theater

Performing Puppets

Giant Puppets

The largest string puppets were first made in Japan. They are called *Bunraku*, and need two or three people to operate them. It takes many years for the operators to master their art. Smaller string puppets are sometimes called *marionettes*. The strings are attached to a small wooden frame. The puppeteer remains hidden from view while he operates the puppets. There may be up to nine strings to work. It is a very skilled job, requiring careful concentration.

Puppet Bodies

A strong puppet must have a firm, but flexible body. Think about the materials you are using — they must be light, but strong. Choose a suitable piece of fabric for the body and attach pieces of yarn or cord. These form the arms and legs. Thread large, heavy buttons to the ends of the strings for hands and feet. For the head shape, either stuff nylon tights with cotton, or make a woolen pom-pom (see page 12). Sew the head to the fabric body.

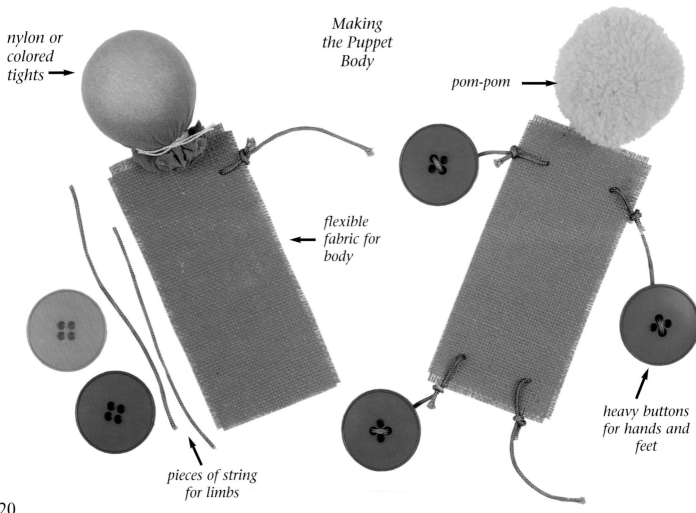

nylon or colored tights →

Making the Puppet Body

pom-pom →

← flexible fabric for body

heavy buttons for hands and feet

pieces of string for limbs

Creating a Character

Once you have made the basic puppet shape, you can decorate it in many ways to turn it into a character. Use material to cover the body and limbs, glueing or sewing them together. Be careful not to make the puppet too stiff — it must always move freely. If you have fabric remnants, wool scraps, buttons, and trimmings, use them imaginatively to create your character.

Cat and Mouse Characters

Control Bar made from craft Sticks

Attaching the Strings

Use a string that is lightweight, but strong. The puppet will need strings attached to all four limbs and one supporting string from the head. Thread strings through the button hands and feet, and sew one to the top of the head. Make sure you have the correct lengths before trimming them. Attach them to a control bar, like the one shown above.

mouse

cat

Rag Rugs

Collecting Rags

In India, particularly in Ahmedabad in Gujarat, women and children collect and sort rags or *chindi* to provide material for the textile industry. The rags are recycled to make artifacts, such as rag rugs, for the local market and for export. Varanasi is well known for its rag rug industry. The rug makers mostly work in their homes using panja looms.

The traditions of rag rug making are international, but all are based on the common idea "waste not, want not." Even scraps of fabric that are too small for practical use can be recycled.

Planning a Rag Rug

You will need to collect a large quantity of different fabrics to make a rug, so start by making a smaller mat to practice. Sort the fabrics into type and color, and make sure they are all clean. Separate plain and patterned materials, and discard any that are too thick. Fine cotton and synthetic fabrics are ideal.

Begin by cutting or tearing the fabrics into long strips. You will be braiding three strips together to make long braids, which will then be coiled and sewn together to make the mat. Think about the color scheme of the finished mat. You may use light colors in the middle and darker shades around the edge.

Braiding

C

B

A

To make a braid, place the left strip A over the middle one B. Then place strip C over A. Repeat these moves until all the fabric is used

Different Braided Effects

Making Braids

Lay the three pieces of fabric on a flat surface and begin braiding them together, as shown opposite. Use a mix of colored and patterned pieces to make different effects. Make a number of these braids, until you use all the fabric.

Coiling and Sewing

The mat is made by coiling the braids into a circular or oval shape, and sewing them into place with strong thread. As the pieces of braid are wound around, new pieces are pinned and sewn in, as shown here. Continue until the mat is finished.

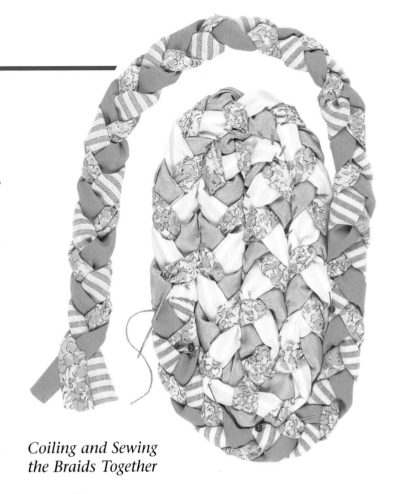

Coiling and Sewing the Braids Together

Finished Coiled Rag Rug

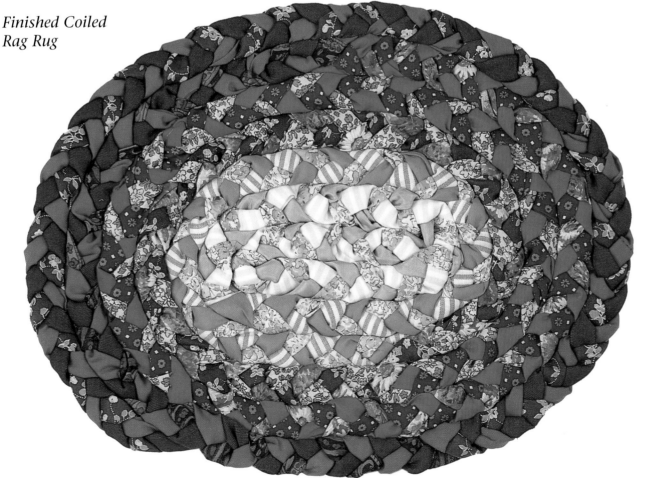

Rag Books

The Meaning of Patchwork

In some societies, the use of discarded items to create something whole has religious meaning. Both Hindus and Buddhists see the patching of cloth as an act of humility. Raffia dance skirts worn by the Kuba women of Africa were often patched. These comma-shaped patches were then turned into a design known as "shina mboa" — the tail of the dog. Here in the United States, patchwork patterns are given names, like Ohio Star. Amish quilts have bold designs.

A Picture of the Past

Articles of clothing can remind us of people and past events. You may look at an old item of clothing and remember the occasion on which it was worn. It might have been a wedding or a birthday celebration. Gather scraps of fabric taken from such garments, and piece them together to create a patchwork history of your family. Design a picture in the form of a family tree. Choose suitable material and make a patch for each member of the family.

Patchwork Family Tree

youngest generation at the top

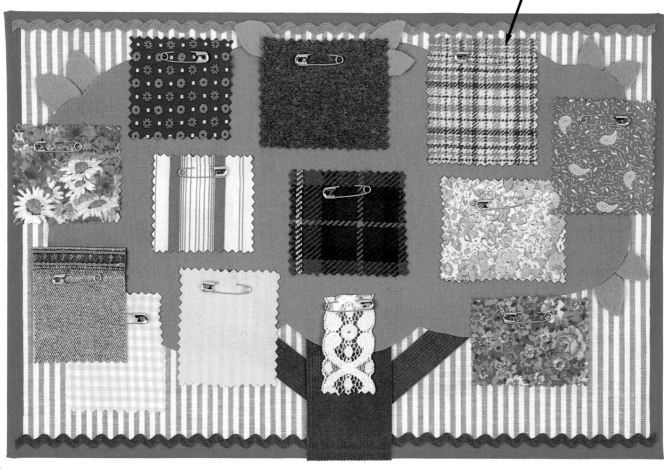

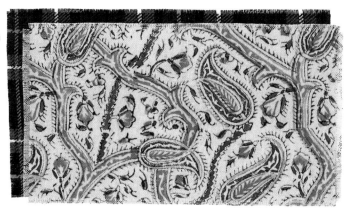

A Patchwork Story

You can make a patchwork story book from your collection. Use pieces of household fabrics, like old curtain and upholstery material, to make the pages of the book. Sew them together using a running stitch. Choose fabrics that remind you of a particular house or room.

Collect scraps of fabric from old clothing belonging to your family. Some of them may have special memories and stories attached to them. Make patch pockets from these pieces of fabric and sew them into the book. Write about the fabrics and the people related to them, and put the stories, with any photographs, inside.

Making a Book from Fabric

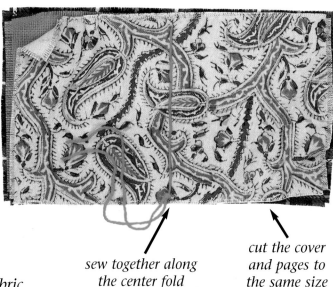

sew together along the center fold

cut the cover and pages to the same size

label for the title

patch pockets containing stories and photographs

New Clothes from Old

Fashionable Clothes

The fashion world is becoming more conscious of the environment. Some designers are choosing fibers like cotton only if they have been grown without the use of pesticides. The finished clothes are expensive, but changes are coming. Tencel is a new fabric that is a mixture of wood pulp and cotton. Remnants of cotton are recycled and turned into paper.

Patching to Create a New Fabric

Patchwork Hat

Patchwork Bag

Fashionable Patching

Some people patch the elbows and knees on clothes, even on new garments, to prevent wear and tear. Sometimes a patchwork effect is used on clothes and bags because it is fashionable.

Lok through your collection of materials and make a new fabric by sewing pieces together. Design and make something useful. Keep your ideas simple and make a paper pattern first as a reference.

Weaving Ties

New and exciting fabrics can be made by weaving old and unwanted items together. Ties very quickly become unfashionable and as a result are discarded. Collect as many colorful, silky ties as you can find. Weave them together to make a brand new fabric.

Weaving Old Ties

Sneaker Bookends

Sneaker Bookends

It is difficult to know what to do with old gym shoes that are worn out or too small. Wash them and then try painting them with acrylic paints. Fill them with stones or plaster to make them heavy and turn them into bookends.

Rag Dolls

Ancient Dolls

Examples of the first rag dolls can still be seen in museums today. One doll that was found in Egypt has been made from a coarse fabric and stuffed with rags.

African Dolls

In some places, such as parts of Africa, children play with toys that they have made at home. Their families are too poor to buy toys from stores, so they make toys from discarded materials. Some of these toys are very intricate. They vary from making models of helicopters, to making simple rag dolls.

Making the Doll

Making a Rag Doll

This rag doll is made from scraps of colored fabric and wool. Make the head by cutting the "foot" from a pair of nylon tights and stuffing it to make a ball shape. Cover the ball with a piece of fabric, tying it tightly at the neck with yarn.

Roll up another piece of fabric to make the arm shape, binding it with yarn at each end to form hands. Divide the fabric at the neck, and tie the arms into place around the waist. This makes the basic doll shape. Tuck extra fabric strips into the waistband.

making the head

attaching the arms

dressing the doll

Worry Dolls

Children of Central America traditionally tell their troubles and worries to tiny dolls before going to sleep at night. These dolls are made from colored threads. There is one doll for each worry. The dolls are placed beneath their pillows, and while they are asleep, the dolls solve all their problems.

Making a Pipe cleaner Body

Make a Family of Worry Dolls and Keep Them in a Drawstring Bag

Making Worry Dolls

You can make your own worry dolls to tell your troubles to. Make the body structures from pipe cleaners, twisting them into shape as shown here. Bind wool around the pipe cleaners, using different colors for the features and clothes. Make a complete family and keep them in a little bag.

← *drawstring bag*

Glossary

Arachne A character from a Greek myth. Her weaving skills so enraged the jealous goddess Athena that she turned arachne into a spider.

Bayeux Tapestry An embroidery 27 in (70 m) long and 18¾ in (48 cm) wide that tells the story of the Norman invasion of Britain in 1066.

Bunraku Style of puppetry that originated in the sixteenth century in Japan. The large string puppets need 3 puppeteers to operate them.

burlap A coarse canvas woven from hemp.

chindi Rags sorted into bundles by Hindu women and children, mainly in Ahmedabad in Gujarat, India. The rags are recycled in textile mills.

durable Able to last for a long time.

fabric Any cloth, woven or nonwoven, made from yarn or fibers.

fibers Natural or synthetic filaments that can be spun into yarn.

flexible Able to bend easily without breaking.

garments Articles of clothing.

genetic engineering When humans interfere with nature by constructing and combining genes.

hem A folded raw edge on a piece of cloth, usually stitched down.

knitting A way of looping and entwining yarn with long, eyeless needles to make shaped pieces of cloth.

loom A frame on which yarn is woven into cloth.

marionettes Puppets with jointed limbs worked by strings.

material Substance of which something is made.

panja looms Devices found in Indian homes and used to weave rag rugs.

remnant A piece of leftover fabric.

synthetic Describes an artificially-made material. The material is made by a chemical reaction.

taut Tightly stretched.

Tencel A brand new textile made from wood pulp and cotton.

threads Strands of material, usually fabric.

warp The lengthwise fixed threads on a loom.

weft Threads woven in and out across the lengthwise warp threads on a loom.

worsted Woolen fabric with a hard, smooth, close-textured surface.

yarn A continuous strand of fibers used in weaving and knitting.

For More Information

Books to Read

Kids Weaving (Projects for Kids of all Ages), Sarah Swett, Stewart, Tabori and Chang, 2005)

Puppet Mania!, John E. Kennedy (North Light Books, 2004)

Puppets (Crafts from Many Cultures), Meryl Doney (Gareth Stevens Publishing, 2004)

My DIY (The Stylin' Girl's Guide to DIY Projects), Kimberley Potts (Adams Media Corporation, 2005)

The Kids Multi-Cultural Craft Book, Roberta Gould (Williamson Publishing Company, 2003)

The Super Duper Art and Craft Activity Book, Lynn Gordon (Chronicle Books, 2005)

Traditional Native American Arts and Activities, Arlette N. Braman (Jossey-Bass, 2000)

Places to Visit

American Textile History Museum,
491 Dutton Street, Lowell, MA 01854

Boston Children's Museum,
300 Congress Street, Boston MA 02210
Includes The Recycle Shop, a children's activity center where re-used materials can be transformed into art projects, and weaving exhibits, including large-scale looms for children to use.)

Frisco Native American Museum and Natural History Center,
Hwy 12, Frisco, NC
Native American artifacts, art and culture)

Metropolitan Museum of Art,
1000 Fifth Avenue. New York, New York 10028
Wide range of exhibits, including jewelry, mosaics, sculpture, block printing, and textiles and dying)

The Long Island Puppet Theatre and Museum,
0 Heitz Place, Hicksville, New York 11801
Puppets from around the world. Performances and puppet making workshops available)

The Noyes Museum,
Lily Lake Road, Oceanville, New Jersey 08231
Collection of folk arts and crafts, including ceramics, jewelery, paper and print, and wood)

Index

Africa 12, 24, 28
    Amish 24
    Central America 29
    Guatemala 13
animalitos 13
Arachne 10

Bayeux Tapestry 14
bookends 27
braiding 22, 23

China 16
collage 5, 7, 9
    abstract 9, 24
    picture 9

decorative items 6, 11
developing countries 4
dolls 28
    African 28
    Egyptian 28
    rag 28
    worry 29

fabrics 4, 5, 8, 9, 10, 12, 22, 25
    burlap 8, 10
    cotton 22, 26
    felt 8, 28
    household 25
    new 26, 27
    nylon 4, 14, 16, 17, 20, 28
    polyester 8, 10, 14, 16
    silk 4, 5, 8, 9, 12, 16
    synthetic 10, 14, 16, 22

Tencel 26
    wool 4, 5, 8, 28, 29
    woolen 5, 10
    worsted 10
fasteners 5, 6, 20, 21
fibers 4, 26
    cotton 4, 5, 10, 26
    linen 4, 10
    silk 4, 5
    wool 4, 5
fleece 4

gloves 5, 18, 19

India 5, 18, 22, 24

Japan 14, 20
    Boys' Festival 14
    puppets 20
    wind socks 14

kites 16, 17
    Chinese 16
    snake 16, 17

Malaysia 12
marionettes 20, 30

patchworks 5, 24, 25, 26
    patterns 24
    quilt 24
    story 24, 25
pesticides 26
pom-poms 12, 20

puppets 18, 19, 20, 21
    Bunraku 20
    control bar 21
    glove 6, 18, 19
    Indian 18
    Japanese 14, 20
string 20, 21
theater 19

quilts 5, 24
    Amish 24
    kanthas 5
    khols 5

rags 4, 5, 22
    chindi 5, 22
    rug 22, 23
recycling 4, 5, 22
remnants 4, 5, 6, 21, 26

socks 5, 6, 18

United States 24

weaving 10, 11, 12, 13
    loom 8, 10, 11
    Sunburst 11
    warp 10
    weft 10, 11
winding yarn 12, 13
wind socks 14, 15
    decorating 15
    dragon-shaped 14
    fish-shaped 14
    Japanese 14